TIME TO SAY GOODBYE

Signs and reasons to give up your relationship with him

ZACHIE GABRIELLA

Table of contents

INTRODUCTION

CHAPTER ONE

YOU ARE INCOMPATIBLE
HE'S INTO SOMETHING
HE LAVISH MONEY A LOT
HE CHEATED ON YOU

CHAPTER TWO

KEEP PRAYING THAT HE WILL CHANGE
HE CAN'T GIVE YOU WHAT YOU NEED
HE WON'T TALK TO YOU
FEELING DEPRESSED AND LONELY
NOTHING YOU SAY OR DO WILL GET YOU BETTER
THERE IS NO "I" IN THIS TEAM

CHAPTER THREE

HE IS SELFISH
YOU HEAR A VOICE IN YOUR HEAD THAT SOMETHING IS WRONG
MUST BEG FOR LOVE AND ATTENTION
YOU HAVE VASTLY DIFFERENT GOALS IN LIFE
YOU KEEP ARGUING ABOUT THE SAME THING

CHAPTER FOUR

You find yourself constantly giving up what you want for what he wants
Scared of him or his reactions
Fear of being alone
He doesn't care how you feel
He is a narcissist

CHAPTER FIVE

You are two very different personalities
His family doesn't kick out *especially mom*
He abuses you
He is emotionally withdrawn
Your relationship is not a priority for him
You are not happy

CHAPTER SIX

CONCLUSION

INTRODUCTION

If you've been questioning yourself, "Should I give him up?" I have good news and bad news for you. The good news is that you still have deep feelings for him. The bad news is that you still have deep feelings for him. Sometimes we fall in love with people who are not good for us. You can love someone deeply even if they aren't good for you or don't give you what you need to feel loved and fulfilled. If you ask "Should I give him up?", then you probably already know the answer. If you are happy and in love, this question will not come to your mind. You are satisfied, satisfied and do not want to break up with him. That said, there's no set timeline for when to dump a guy. Every relationship is different, so ultimately you need to follow your own gut. So, if you're still wondering about the signs that you should cancel, here are some things to keep in mind. Let's preface everything that follows by saying that there is no such thing as a perfect human being. It's hard for all girls to accept, but no one is perfect. But don't just miss the minor irritants. The time will come. If you feel like you're sacrificing something important or necessary for someone in your life, it may be love, but that's not the right thing to do. We all experience ups and downs in relationships. When valleys are hard to climb and mountains aren't too high, you should stop and ask yourself why you're staying. As with the net equation, good times should outweigh bad times. . Otherwise it's not worth wasting your life.

CHAPTER ONE

You are incompatible

Incompatibility is very difficult to overcome in a relationship. For example, let's say one of your girlfriends is extrovert and the other is an introvert/domestic.

Extroverts want to go out, do fun things, and meet other people. Introverts, on the other hand, don't like to leave the house and don't like socializing. These personalities are very incompatible. So think again if you two are compatible.

He's into something

Addiction should also be viewed as a deal breaker. When we think of addiction, we usually think of alcohol and drugs. But there are many other addictions that can damage relationships. It could be an addiction to pornography, video games, or gambling. Addiction takes his attention away from you and the relationship.

He lavish money a lot

Financial issues are the one of the main reasons couples break up. If one of you is a saver and the other a saver, you don't work well together. Maybe he gambles, does things with his money that you don't approve of, or doesn't ask for your opinion. This can be a big problem in relationships.

He cheated on you

Cheating and betrayal should also be a deal-breaker, but not for many. Some women give the cheater too many chances but continue to cheat. Whether it's cheating or some other kind of betrayal, it's unlikely to change, so you should seriously consider giving up.

CHAPTER TWO

Keep praying that he will change

If you keep praying for things to change between the two of you, really pray for him to change, there is one thing he absolutely knows is true in this world. It seems that the only person you can change is yourself.

If he isn't what you want or need, or doesn't provide what you need to feel complete, he will never.

He can't give you what you need

The hardest part is realizing that the person you love is not what you need and will never need. When investing in someone, it can sometimes seem selfish to want more than they offer you. The problem is that you can only start once in your life. Don't spend your life regretting that you weren't with someone who didn't make your life happy and fulfilling.

He won't talk to you

You cannot be in a relationship with someone who does not speak or communicate with you. If he finds it irritating to talk about problems, runs away from you and conflict, or thinks you can't sit down and have a civilized conversation about your life's problems, then you can have a peaceful union. You can't. Unreasonable people will always remain unreasonable. They run and you chase them forever. You may not think you're giving up, but stop chasing.

Feeling depressed and lonely

If you feel depressed and lonely all the time, you need to let go and move on. There is nothing worse than feeling lonely with someone. At some point, ask yourself if you'd rather have him or not. What exactly is he doing other than making you feel stuck and constantly waiting for him to show up and be the person you need?

Nothing you say or do will get you better

No matter what you say or do, things will never be resolved. Do you know why? Because he doesn't want it. Say things like "I just don't want to argue" but either run away from you, leave you out and let you down, or consistently say the exact thing he knows hurts the most. If anyone does it, that's it. Is it on purpose? It's not that he doesn't know how you feel. He doesn't care. Don't let him sit and wait for someone he doesn't care about you.

There is no "I" in this team

If he wants his life to be his life, that doesn't change. He may have learned to keep secrets and live separate lives through his parents' relationships, but in reality, such relationships make you who you are. If you're together and he still has it all to himself, that won't change.

CHAPTER THREE

He is selfish

Selfish people don't change. Waiting for him to grow up and act mature, but if he waits too long, it's not maturity, he's a selfish man. You can't date someone who thinks only of himself.

You hear a voice in your head that something is wrong

That little voice in our heads is, yeah, a slut! But do you know what else she is? She is honest most of the time. She hates to put up with what her head is saying because her heart says otherwise, but that inner voice is always right. It is your soul that is telling you that something should not be.

Must beg for love and attention

If you're begging for his love and attention, you deserve better. If someone ignores you or pays no attention to you, it's a lack of respect. You don't want to live your life with someone who doesn't believe in you.

You have vastly different goals in life

If he wants to climb the corporate ladder and live a life without kids and travel, stop thinking he'll change his mind once he finds out what you want. , if you want to have a picket fence, this may not be the place for you. It's not fair to want him to give up his goals in life. But giving up isn't fair either. So if they don't merge, don't give up. It's realistic and will save you a lifetime of strife and heartbreak.

You keep arguing about the same thing

If you're arguing about the same thing as you were 10 years ago, you'll never stop arguing about it. There are things in a relationship that can't be reconciled. If you try to meet him halfway and he doesn't budge, or if you can't forgive him despite your attempts, it's time to let go and move on. It's okay to say

"I can't do this anymore" at the end.

CHAPTER FOUR

You find yourself constantly giving up what you want for what he wants

If so, trust us. If you make sacrifices now, they will always be. The reason you give up and give up is that you learned it. It doesn't change. When you finally stand up for yourself, it doesn't get better. He won't like it.

Scared of him or his reactions

If you're afraid of him or his response, it's time to go. No one in a relationship should scare you. Either he's withholding love, being physically abusive, or you're scared and just following along, the answer to your question, "Should I give him up?" is harsh. Yes!

Fear of being alone

At some point, you have to ask yourself why you never give up, even if you are asking yourself that question.

You may just be afraid of being alone or that no one else will come. Trust us, someone will. There is always another relationship around the corner. And even if this is not suitable, a suitable one will appear.

He doesn't care how you feel

If he really doesn't care that you're crying in front of him, or if you're in trouble and he won't come to your aid, walk away. You can't teach someone to take care of you. You can't push him, and you certainly can't keep begging for it. If he doesn't care about your feelings, let go.

He is a narcissist

A narcissist thinks only of one person: himself. If he runs up to you every time you start walking but refuses to acknowledge your presence when you're by his side, then you're dealing with a personality style that many don't survive. Run now while your self-esteem is still intact. Narcissists don't change because they can't. They lacked empathy, so they couldn't do it even if they wanted to.

CHAPTER FIVE

You are two very different personalities

If you are a "kind" person and he is the "I don't fuck" type, you will both always have misunderstandings. The peace you crave is not there. Personality styles don't change the way you want them to. If you come as far as you can and he does too, but you still can't meet in the middle of being happy, you'll never be happy.

*His family doesn't kick out *especially mom**

If his family is the main point of contention in your relationship, that doesn't change, if he runs to his mom every time he has a problem, or if his family doesn't like you and nobody If we're talking about you, it's a coffin nail. He encourages it and never quits.

He abuses you

Abuse in a relationship should be an instant deal-breaker for anyone...but there are many types of abuse beyond physical abuse. Emotional and emotional abuse is just as harmful in very different ways. So if he puts his hands on you, hits you, knocks you down, or mentally torments you, it's time to give up on him - he will never change.

He is emotionally withdrawn

If a man is always "in his own world" and never engages with you, he is emotionally withdrawn. The point is, if he's not emotionally connected to you, it's not a satisfying relationship.

Your relationship is not a priority for him

If he finds out that he puts almost all of his life before you, then you are not his first priority in life. Dating his guy friends, working, drinking, and videoing his games may be more important to him than you.

You are not happy

This seems so easy, and that's probably the number one reason you should end it. If you're not happy with him, what other options do you have? After all, the goal in life should be happiness. If he's sucking the joy out of your life, why are you with him in the first place? There are other people who can put a smile on your face.

CHAPTER SIX

CONCLUSION

The decision to break up with a loved one is one of the most difficult decisions in the world. If no matter how you approach the relationship, it's not giving you what you want, it's time to let go and move on. It's not about giving up on him, it's about realizing that you might not be the best for each other. Abandoning him means that if you hold out long enough, he will change. So be careful, it will hurt, but

the sun will rise tomorrow.
You will find your new normal
and someone who will provide
what you need from the start
so you don't have to ask if you
should skip hello.

www.ingramcontent.com/pod-product-compliance
Lightning Source LLC
LaVergne TN
LVHW020537160826
845677LV00015B/4113

* 9 7 9 8 3 5 6 6 6 3 5 4 3 *